PEARLS OF LIFE

COLLECTION OF 100 AMAZING SHORT STORIES

JOSEPH M THOHRII

Made with ♥ on the Notion Press Platform
www.notionpress.com

Fondly Remembered

This book is lovingly dedicated to beloved
Late A. Mada-a Margaret
(1940-2024)
New Makhan Village, Senapati District,
Manipur
Eldest Sister of Mrs. Sania Philomena
Sister in law of Mr. J.K. Makabo
Aunt of Fr. Joseph Thohrii,
Dr. Michael Shulee, Mario Mulee
Moses Loshu & David Ariijii.
Her life was a blessing to us all and whose motherly love, care and sacrifice made us the person we are today.
May her soul Rest in Peace.

Contents

Contents

Contents

Contents

Preface

"Authors do not choose a story to write, the story chooses us". (Richard P. Denney)

Human civilization has always been a part of the era of human history. And we are privileged today to be part of that history which will inspire the future generations in one way or the other. Each history has stories and even anecdotes that impart lessons, values, morals and above all inspiration to be looked up upon by the coming generations. Stories can be a powerful tool for personal growth and can inspire us to take action. They can help us believe in our potential to achieve success and face challenges with courage. Stories can also help us recommit to our vision and remind us that success is the result of hard work, dedication and resilience.

The stories and anecdotes in my book **Pearls of Life** here have been edited and reproduced from various sources on varied subjects. These stories and anecdotes have really motivated and inspired me in my life's journey and I believe it will motivate and inspire the readers of these collections as I was. I regret that I could not produce all references and make due acknowledgment of the collections presented in my book. Most of them are by anonymous writers however, I am indebted to all the authors whose contributions are used. I will remain ever grateful to all who have encouraged and helped me in compiling these collections.

I remain ever grateful to **Shri Kereilhouvi Angami IFS (Retd.)**, former Principal Chief Conservator of Forests & Head of Forest Force, Govt. of Manipur, for readily accepting my request to write the Forward of my book.

Thank you very much.

Joseph M Thohrii
The Compiler

Foreword

In the realm of literature, brevity often holds the most profound truths. Pearls of Life, a collection of '100 Amazing Short Stories' invites readers into a world where every word counts, and each narrative is a snapshot of human experience, which inspires, entertains and enlightens. Handpicked by a Catholic Priest, these tales weave together timeless moral lessons, heartfelt reflections on faith, clever humour, and cherished anecdotes from everyday life. The stories within these pages are crafted to be consumed quickly, yet they will linger in the mind long after the last sentence is read.

Through these stories, readers are invited to reflect on the human condition, exploring themes of love, loss and the intricacies of daily life. Perfect for readers of all ages, this book serves as a well-spring of hope and guidance, offering nuggets of truth to ponder in moments of doubt or joy. Whether you seek a smile, a spark of inspiration, or a deeper understanding of life's meaning, Pearls of Life promises to leave a lasting and lingering impression in our heart and soul.

As you delve into the 100 Amazing short stories, prepare to embark on a journey that is both entertaining and enlightening. Each story is a portal of fleeting moment captured in words that invites you to pause, reflect and perhaps even see your own life through a new lens. This collection is not just a book, it is an experience that celebrates the art of storytelling in its most distilled form. In a fast – paced world, let these stories remind us of the beauty found in brevity and the power of a well told tale. Pearls of Life is an everyday reminder that even in life's smallest moments, great wisdom can be found and experienced.

My heartiest congratulation to Rev. Fr. Joseph Makabo Thohrii, and may God's Grace & Mercy be upon us all.

(Kereilhouvi Angami) IFS (Retd)
Medziphema, Nagaland

Chapter 1

Love Trampled

There was a blind girl who hated herself just because she was blind. She hated everyone, except her loving friend. He was always there for her. He cared for her and helped her a lot as she was blind. It was a very sincere love. One day, she said that if she could only see the world, she would marry her friend and it was her great desire. Her friend tried a lot and worked for the medical expenses.

One day someone donated a pair of eyes to her and then she could see everything, including her boyfriend. Her boyfriend asked her, "Now that you can see the world, will you marry me?"

The girl was shocked when she saw that her boyfriend was blind too, and refused to marry him. Her boyfriend walked away in tears, and later wrote a letter to her saying: "Just take care of my eyes dear."

Chapter 2

Help Others Win

A few years ago at the Seattle Special Olympics, nine contestants, all physically or mentally disabled, assembled at the starting line for the 100 yard dash. At the sound of the gun, they all started out, not exactly in a dash, but with a relish to run the race to the finish and win. All, that is, except one who stumbled on the asphalt, tumbled over a couple of times and began to cry.

The other eight heard the boy. They slowed down and looked back. They all turned around and went back. Everyone of them. One girl with Down's syndrome bent down, kissed him, and said, "This will make it better." All nine linked arms and walked across the finish line together. Everyone in the stadium stood, and the cheering went on for several minutes.

Chapter 3

Temper Control

There once was a little boy who had a bad temper. His father gave him a bag of nails and told him that every time he lost his temper, he must hammer a nail into the fence.

The first day the boy had driven 37 nails into the fence. Over the next few weeks as he learned to control his anger, the number of nails hammered daily, gradually dwindled down. He discovered it was easier to hold his temper than to drive those nails into the fence. Finally the day came when the boy didn't lose his temper at all. He told his father about it and the father suggested that the boy now pull out nails for each day that he was able to hold his temper.

The day passed and the young boy was finally able to tell his father that all the nails were gone. The father took his son by the hand and led him to the fence. He said, "You have done well, my son but look at the holes in the fence. The fence will never be the same. When you say things in anger, they leave a scar just like this one."

You can put a knife in a man and draw it out. It will not matter how many times you say "I'm sorry", the wound is still there.

Make sure you control your temper the next time you are tempted to say something in anger you remember you will regret later.

Chapter 4

True Friend

Horror gripped the heart of the World War I solider as he saw his lifelong friend fall in battle. Caught in a trench with continuous gunfire whizzing over his head, the solider asked his lieutenant if he might go out into the "no man's land" between the trenches to bring his fallen comrade back.

"You can go" said the lieutenant, "but I don't think it will be worth it. Your friend is probably dead and you may throw your life away". The solider went anyway. Miraculously he managed to reach his friend, hoist him onto his shoulder and brought him back to their company's trench. As the two of them tumbled in together to the bottom of the trench, the officer checked the wounded soldier, and then looked kindly at his friend. "I told you it wouldn't be worth it," he said." "Your friend is dead and you are mortally wounded." "What do you mean; worth it?" responded the lieutenant. "Your friend is dead."

"Yes, sir" the private answered. "But it was worth it because when I got to him, he was still alive and I had the satisfaction of hearing him saying, "Jim……, I knew you'd come."

Chapter 5

A Simple Gesture

Mark was walking home from school one day when he noticed the boy ahead of him had tripped and dropped all of the books he was carrying, along with two sweaters, a baseball bat, a glove and a small tape recorder. Mark knelt down and helped the boy pick up the scattered articles. Since they were going the same way, he helped to carry part of the burden. As they walked Mark discovered the boy's name was Bill, that he loved video games, baseball and history, and that he was having lots of trouble with other subjects and that he had just broken up with his girlfriend.

They arrived at Bill's home first and Mark was invited in for a coke and to watch some Television. The afternoon passed pleasantly with a few laughs and shared some talk, and then Mark went home. They continued to see each other once or twice, they both graduated from Juniors High School. They ended up in the same High School where they had brief contacts over the years.

Finally, the long awaited senior year came and three weeks before graduation, Bill asked Mark if they could talk.

Bill reminded him of the day years ago when they had first met. "Did you ever wonder why I was carrying so many things home that day?" asked Bill. "You see, I cleaned out my locker because I didn't want to leave a mess for anyone else. I had stored away some of my mother's sleeping pill and I was going home to commit suicide. But after we spent some time together talking and laughing, I realized that if I had killed myself, I would have missed that time and so many others might follow. So you know Mark, when you picked up those books that day, you did a lot more, you saved my life."

Chapter 6

Paid in Full With A Glass of Milk

One day a poor boy who was selling goods from door to door to pay his way through school, found he had only one thin dime left, and he was hungry. He decided he would ask for a meal at the next house. However, he lost his nerve when a lovely young woman opened the door. Instead of a meal he asked for a drink of water. She thought he looked hungry so brought him a large glass of milk. He drank it slowly, and then asked, “How much do I owe you?” “You don’t owe me anything,” she replied. “Mother has taught us never to accept pay for a kindness”. He said, “Then I thank you from my heart.”

As Howard Kelly left that house, he not only felt stronger physically, but his faith in God and man was strong too. He had been ready to give up and quit.

Years later, that young woman became critically ill. The local doctor was baffled. They finally sent her to the big city, where they called in specialists to study her rare disease. Dr. Howard Kelly was called in for the consultation. When he heard, the name of the town she came from, a strange light filled his eyes. Immediately he rose and went down the hall of the hospital to her room. Dressed in his doctor’s gown he went in to see her. He recognized her at once. He went back to the consultation room determined to do his best to save her life. From that day, he gave special attention to the case. After a long struggle, the battle was won. Dr. Kelly requested the business office to pass the final bill to him for approval. He looked at it, and then wrote something on the edge and the bill was sent to her room. She feared to open it, for she was sure it would take the rest of her life to pay for it all. Finally she looked, and something caught her attention on the side of the bill. She began to read the following words:”Paid in full with one glass of milk”.

Chapter 7

Behind Every Successful man there is a Great Woman

Joseph Parker, CEO of the Massachusetts Mutual Life Insurance Company, and his wife, Maria were driving along an interstate highway when he noticed that the car was low on gas. Parker got off the highway at the next exit and soon found a rundown gas station with just one gas pump. He asked the lone attendant to fill the tank and check the oil, and then he went for a little walk around the station to stretch his leg.

As he was returning to the car, he noticed that the attendant and his wife were engaged in an animated conversation. The conversation stopped as he paid the attendant, But he was getting back into the car, he saw the attendant wave and heard him say, "It was great talking to you".

As he drove out of the station, Parker asked his wife if she knew the man. She readily admitted she did. They had gone to High School together and had dated steadily for about a year.

"Maria you were lucky that I came along?" bragged Parker. "If you had married him, you'd be the wife of a gas station attendant instead of the wife of a Chief Executive Officer".

"My dear", replied his wife, "If I had married him, he'd be the Chief Executive Officer and you'd be the Gas station attendant."

Chapter 8

Write on Sand or Stone?

A story tells that two friends were walking through the desert. During some point of the journey, they had an argument, and one friend slapped the other one in the face. The one who got slapped was hurt, but without saying anything, he wrote in the sand: Today my best friend slapped me in the face.

They kept on walking, until they found an Oasis, where they decided to take a bath. The one who had been slapped got stuck in the mire and started drowning, but his friend saved him. After he recovered from the near drowning, he wrote on a stone: Today my best friend saved my life.

The friend, who had slapped and saved his best friend, asked him, "After I hurt you, you wrote in the sand, and now you write on a stone, why?"

The other friend replied: "When someone hurts us, we should write it down in sand, where the winds of forgiveness can erase it away, but when someone does something good for us, we must engrave it in stone where no wind can ever erase it. Learn to write your hurts in the sand and to carve your blessings in stone.

Chapter 9

Four wives in our lives.

Once upon a time, a rich King had four wives. He loved the fourth wife the most, adorned her with rich robes, and treated her to the finest of delicacies. He gave her nothing but the best.

He also loved the third wife very much and was always showing her off to neighboring kingdoms. However, he feared that one day she would leave him for another.

He also loved his second wife. She was his confident and was always kind, considerate and patient with him. Whenever, the king faced a problem, he could confide in her, and she would help him get through the difficult times.

The king's first wife was a very loyal partner and had made great contribution in maintaining his wealth and kingdom. However, he did not love the first wife. Although she loved him deeply, he hardly took notice of her!

One day the king fell ill and he knew his time was short. He thought of his luxurious life and wondered. "I now have four wives with me, but when I die, I'll be all alone"

Thus he asked the fourth wife, 'I have loved you the most, endowed you with the finest clothing and showered great care for you. Now that I'm dying, will you follow me and keep me company?"

"No way!" replied the fourth wife and she walked away without another word.

Her answer cut like a sharp knife right into his heart. The sad king then asked the third wife, "I have loved you all my life. Now that I'm dying, will you follow me and keep me company?"

"No!" replied the third wife. 'Life is too good! When you die, I'm going to remarry!" His heart sank and turned cold.

He then asked the second wife, "I have always turned to you for help and you've always been there for me. When I die, will you follow me and keep me company?"

"I' m sorry, I can't help you out this time!" replied the second wife. "At the very most, I can only accompany you to your grave". Her answer came like a bolt of lightning, and the king was devastated.

Then a voice called out; "I'll leave with you and follow up, and there was his first wife. She was so skinny as she suffered from malnutrition and neglect.

Greatly grieved, the king said, "I should have taken much better care of you when I had the chance!"

In truth, we all have four wives in our lives: Our fourth wife is our body. No matter how much time and effort we lavish in making it look good or feel good, it will leave us when we die.

Our third wife is our possessions, status and wealth. When we die, it will all go to others.

Our second wife is our family and friends. No matter how much they have been for us, the furthest they can stay by us is up to the grave.

In addition, our first wife is our Soul. Often neglected in pursuit of wealth, power and pleasure of the world.

However, our soul is the only thing that will follow us wherever we go. Cultivate, strengthen and cherish it now, for it is the only part of us that will follow us to the throne of God and continue with us throughout eternity.

Chapter 10

The Priest and the Parishioners

An old priest and some of his parishioners were waiting to be admitted to heaven. Every hour, St Peter would call a name, indicating that it was the persons turn to enter paradise.

Repeatedly, to the priest's dismay someone else's name was called until he was the only one standing outside the pearly gates.

Finally, he heard his name and he stepped inside briskly. He wasted no time in voicing out his complaint to St. Peter. "How come I was the last to be called?" he asked. Don't you know that I am the Parish Priest? Without me none of my parishioners would be here! What have they done in my parish that entitled them to enter heaven ahead of me?"

Grinning gleefully, St. Peter replied, "They prayed that you would be faithful to your calling."

Chapter 11

Stories told by my Mother

Kuttyamma was the mother of the wealthiest man in the village. She was proud of her son's achievement. All in the village know the son as a loving, generous and kind man. He owned three mansions like buildings and many small servant quarter. But Kuttayamma lived in a small hut like house. To everyone who asked her why she does not go to her son's house she replies, "This is the house I was born, this is the house my father died, this the house I was married, this the house my mother died, this is the house my children were born, this the house my husband died and this is the house in which I want to die". But the truth is that her son's wife had called Kuttyamma's husband- an old man of eighty plus- "a dirty swine" because he unknowingly touch the wall of her big mansion with his faltering hands and the wall was dirtied. He told Kuttyammma, "Our little hut is much better than this big mansion".

When Kuttyammma's husband died the son arranged a grand funeral. The whole village attended it, not because of sympathy but because of the food served after the funeral. Kuttyamma mourned the death of her husband as a faithful wife.

The son's fame was increasing day by day and Kuttyamma did her level best to keep up to the standard of her son. Every pie she could manage was spent on the house. She painted it, curtained it and beautified it. No one should say that Kuttyamma's son did not look after her well.

Kuttyamma became ill and too old to do any work. The village people told the son that Kuttyamma was sick and old. The son sent a doctor to give her regular check-up and medicine. The doctor did his duty faithfully. He visited her every month and gave the prescription for the medicine. Kuttyamma kept the prescription under the pillow. Month after month it got piled up. One day the doctor asked her "Why are you becoming very feeble and thin? Are you not taking the medicine?" She looked at him pathetically. But said nothing.

A few days later Kuttyamma died. Her son came to arrange a big funeral. While placing the body in the coffin he found a letter among the prescriptions, "My dear son" it read, I have tried to live worthy of your reputation. Without food and without medicine I lived. All the prescription are under the pillow... I am sad I have to disappoint you in death. I could not help but die like this... He felt his body sinking under a heavy weight. He left the room with his head bent without looking at the waiting crowd.

Chapter 12

You Cannot Please Everyone

Once a man and his little son packed necessary things for a two-day trip on their donkey. The boy was leading the donkey and the father was coming behind, encouraging the animal with a little stick. A man in the village saw them walking and told the father, 'what are you walking for'? You have a donkey with you, sit on it and give your feet some rest. Donkey are for carrying people and they are strong. So both of them sat on the donkey and continued their journey. On the way the policeman stopped them and said, one of you better get down, otherwise I will arrest you for cruelty of the animal. So the father got down and walk along. As they were going they came upon an elderly man. He saw the father walking and the young boy sitting on the donkey, Aren't you ashamed of yourself? A strong boy like you sitting on the donkey and allowing your father, an old man walking and out of breath. Get down from the donkey and allow your father to sit.

The boy got down and made his father to sit on the donkey. Then a farmer saw this and shouted at the father, aren't you ashamed? You have long legs, why don't you walk, you are making this poor little boy to walk all the way with you. No matter what the two of them did, everyone criticized. Finally they carried the donkey and the people thought they were really stupid and laughed at them.

MORAL: No matter what you do, what you are or who you are, people will have reasons to criticize and make fun. Therefore, don't bother with what other think of you, just be true to yourself.

Chapter 13

Thought To Ponder… Where Do You Stand?

Once Bill Gates and his son went to a restaurant. After eating, Bill Gates gave $5 to the waiter as a tip. The waiter had a strange feeling on his face after the tip. Gates realized and asked, what happened? The waiter said, "I'm just amazed because on the same table your son gave tip of …$500… and you his father, richest man in the world gave $5 only?"

Gates smiled and replied in these words: "He is son of the world's richest man, but I am the son of a wood cutter…"

Moral: Never forget your past. It is your best teacher. Hard-earned money will be spent after much calculation. Ill-gotten money will be wasted anyhow. Be careful, how you earn your money.

Chapter 14

The Most Remembered Teacher

Dr. A.P.J. Abdul Kalam, the former President of India visited Loyola Institute of Business Administration on the occasion of its silver Jubilee celebrations. After having a meaningful interaction with the students, he passed through Loyola College. As he came near the Church in the President convoy, somebody informed him that there was the cemetery of Fathers and Brothers who worked for Loyola College, buried there, Rev. Fr. T.M. Sequeria SJ was also buried there. As soon as he heard the name of the father, he jumped out of the car putting the security men in disarray. He went straight to the grave of the Father and knelt down before it and kissed it.

Dr. Kalam regarded Fr.Sequeira as one of his beloved teacher who made a deep impression on his life and also made the most and positive intervention when he was an undergraduate student of St. Joseph's college, living in the new hostel. He went through the most critical time when his father lost the only boat they had for livelihood. Dr. Kalam could not pay the college fees. Every day, Fr. Sequeira met him, encouraged him and helped him financially to complete his degree and referred him to a distinguished professor at the Madras Institute of Technology, Guindy.

That was the starting point of the brilliant career of Dr. Kalam. He knelt in front of the grave and said these beautiful words:

"Fr.Sequeira if you are not there, there is no Abdul Kalam.

Fr.Sequeira if you are not there, there is no nuclear scientist called Abdul Kalam.

Fr.Sequeira if you are not there, there is no Bharat Ratna Abdul Kalam.

Fr.Sequeira if you are not there, there is no President Abdul Kalam."

This is the glowing tribute a student can pay to his teacher. This is the way he showed esteem and reverence to his teacher who touched his life. He has referred this in his autobiography, *The Wings of Fire.*

Chapter 15

Life's Lesson From the Pencil

A pencil maker told the pencils five important lessons.
Firstly, everything you do will always leave a mark.
Secondly, but you can always correct the mistakes you make.
Thirdly, what is important is what is inside you.
Fourthly, in life you will undergo painful sharpening which will make you a better pencil.
And fifthly, to be the best pencil you can be, you must allow yourself to be held and guided by the hands that holds you.
Dear readers, may you be the best God's pencil and let his mighty hands guide you always throughout your life.

Chapter 16

What Is Faith, Trust and Hope?

Once all the villagers decided to pray for rain. On the day of prayer, all people gathered , but only one boy came with an umbrella. That is Faith!

When you throw babies in the air, they laugh because they know you will catch them. That is Trust

Every night we go to bed without any assurance of being alive the next morning, but still we set alarms to wake up. That is Hope!

We plan big things for tomorrow in spite of zero knowledge of the future. That is confidence!

We see the world suffering, but still, we get married and have children. That is love!

On an old man's shirt was written a sentence 'I am not 80 years old: I am sweet 16 with 64 years of experience', That is attitude!

Never lose your Faith, Trust and Hope.

Chapter 17

What Bible Says About You?

Ruth was a widow but God made her a mother,
Esther was a foreigner but God made her a queen,
Daniel was a slave but God made him a Prime Minister,
David was a forgotten shepherd but God made him a king,
Moses was a failure but God made him a leader,
Peter was a failure but God made him a forceful preacher and
Paul was a murderer but God made him a powerful apostle.
Remember there is so much in you that God wants to bring out from you.
Yield to Him and be blessed.

Chapter 18

Gravity Doesn't Care!

We might need one potato and a pencil. Let's start. Hold both the two items together between your two palm, released it at the same time. Observe carefully. Now tell which one would hit the ground first? The potato or the pencil?

Many of us will think that potato would hit first as it is heavier than pencil. But it's not. Both of them hit at the same time. You might get wonder but it's true. Why?

Let's see, the earth itself act as a big magnet. It pulls everything on earth with the same gravitational force. So how big and heavier the potato is, it hit the ground at the same time with the pencil. Galileo, the person who discovered it, called the "equivalent principle".

Likewise God love us all. Whether you are big, small, fat, thin, slim, beautiful, ugly, handsome, black, white, rich, poor, he draws us equally towards him and want to have a relationship to everyone. In his eyes we all are same. Paul state in Galatians 3:28 "You are all one in Christ Jesus". See how wonderful and nice it is to be loved by God with same value as he loved others!"

Chapter 19

Good Night or Good Bye

Dr. Langdale of New York tells us of a devoted Christian businessman who was stuck by an automobile and hurried to a hospital. He was informed he had only two hours to live. His faith was implicit in the goodness of God hereafter. He had called his family to him and thus addressed them: "Goodnight, dear wife. Through sunshine and shadow we have walked together. You have been my inspiration in everything I have undertaken. Many times I have seen the spirit of God shining in your face. I'll love you far more than the day you became my bride. Good night dear, I'll see you in the morning, Goodnight". "Good night, Mary. You are our first born. What a joy you have been to you father. What a Christian you are Mary; you will never forget how your father loved you. Goodnight, Mary, Goodnight."

"Goodnight, Will (He turned to his eldest son). Will, your coming into our home had been unmixed blessing. You love the God of your father. You will continue to grow in every Christian grace and virtue. You are your father's love and blessing. Good night, Will, Good night".

Goodnight, Gracie" (Charlie had fallen under evil influences and grievously disappointed his father and mother. The dying man skipped him and spoke to the youngest child, a beautiful young girl).

"Gracie, you have long been a song of gladness, a ray of light. When not long ago you surrendered your life into Christ, your father's cup of Happiness was full to overflown. Goodnight, little girl, Goodnight".

"Goodbye Charlie, He then called Charlie to his side. "Charlie, what a fine, promising boy you were. Your father and mother believed you would develop into a noble man. We gave you all the opportunities we gave to the other children. If there had been any differences, you yourself must admit that difference was all in your own favour. You have disappointed us. You have followed the bad and downward road. You have not heeded the warnings of God's Holy word. You have not hearkened to the call of the saviour. However, I have always love you and love you still, Charlie.

God only knows how much I love you. Goodbye, Charlie, Goodbye".

Charlie seized his father's hand and between sobs he cried out, "Father, why have you said Goodnight to the others and Goodbye to me?"

"For the simple reason that I shall meet the other members of the family 'in the morning', but by all the promises that assure us of a reunion, by those same statement of God's word, I can have no hope of seeing you 'over there'. Goodbye, Charlie, Goodbye".

Charlie fell on his knee by his father's bed and cried out in agony of his soul, praying God to forgive his sins.

"Do you mean, Charlie, are you in earnest?"

"God knows I am", said the heartbroken young man.

"Then God will hear you and save you, Charlie, and it is Goodnight and not Goodbye. Goodnight Charlie, and it is goodnight and not Goodbye. Goodnight Charlie, Goodnight my boy". And he was gone.

Charlie is now a preacher of the Gospel.

Chapter 20

Live and Work

Father was a hardworking man who delivered bread as living to support his wife and three children. He spent all his evenings after work attending classes, hoping to improve himself so that he could one day find a better paying job. Except for Sundays, Father hardly ate a meal together with his family. He worked and studied very hard because he wanted to provide his family with the best things he could buy.

Whenever the family complained that he was not spending enough time with them, he reasoned that he was doing all this for them. However, he often yearned to spend more time with the family. The day came when the examination result were announced. To his joy, Father passed, and with distinctions too! Soon after he was offered a good job as a senior supervisor which paid handsomely.

Like a dream come true, father could now afford to provide his family with life's little luxuries like nice clothing, fine food and vacation abroad.

However, the family still did not get to see father for most of the week. He continued to work very hard, hoping to be promoted to the position of manager. In fact, to make himself a worthily candidate for promotion he enrolled for another course in the Open University.

Again, whenever the family complained that he was not spending enough time with them, he reasoned that he was doing all this for them. But often yearned to spend more time with the family. Father's hard work paid off and he was promoted. Jubilantly, he decided to hire a maid to relieve his wife from her domestic tasks. He also felt that their three-room flat was no longer big enough; it would be nice for his family to be able to enjoy the facilities and comfort of a condominium. Having experienced the reward of his hard work many times before, Father resolved to further his studies and work at being promoted again. The family still did not get to see much of him. In fact, sometimes father had to work on Sundays entertaining clients. Again, whenever the family complained that he was not spending enough time with them, he reasoned that he was doing all this for them. But he often yearned to spend more time with his family.

As expected, Father's hard work paid off again and he bought a beautiful condominium overlooking the coast of Singapore. On the first Sunday evening at their new home, father declared to his family that he decided not to take anymore course or pursue anymore promotion from then on he was going to devote more time to his family.

Father did not wake up the next day.

Chapter 21

Change Yourself

Once upon a time, there was a king who ruled a prosperous country. One day, he went for a trip to some distant areas of his country. When he came back to his palace, he complained that his feet were very painful, because it was the first time that he went for such a long trip, and the road that he went through was very rough and stony. He then ordered his people to cover every road of the entire country with leather.

Definitely, this would need thousands of cow's skin, and would cost a huge amount of money.

Then one of his wise servants dared himself to tell the king, "Why do you have to spend that unnecessary amount of money? Why don't you just cut a little piece of leather to cover your feet?"

The king was surprised, but he later agreed to his suggestion, to make a "shoe" for himself.

There is actually a valuable lesson of life in this story; to make this world a happy place to live in, you better change yourself-your heart; and not the world.

Chapter 22

Being Available

A small candle was carried by a man who was climbing the stairs of a lighthouse. On their way up, the candle asked the man, "Where are we going?"

"We're going to the top of this lighthouse and give signals to the big ships on the ocean," the man answered. "What? How could it be possible for me with my small light to give signals to those big ships?"

"They will never be able to see my light", replied the candle weakly.

"That's your part. If your light is small, let it be. All you have to do is keep burning and leave the rest to me", said the man.

A little later, they arrived at the top of the lighthouse where there was a big lamp. Then the man lit the lamp with the light of the candle and instantly, the place shone so brightly that the ships on the ocean could see its light.

Very often in life we are worried about our limitations and we stay away from allowing God to use us. God does not look at our abilities or inabilities. He is only looking for our availability. You should bear in mind that your life is like a small candle in God's most powerful hand. All your abilities and expertise will remain as small as the small candle unless you make yourself available to God. On the contrary, even if your light is just a small flicker, if you surrender your life to God, He will make use of it most meaningfully in a mighty and just way that will bring blessings to many people.

Chapter 23

Overcoming

Adam Bender is an amazing example of the value of overcoming. In his words, he says: "My name is Adam Bender, I am a 10 year old cancer survivor, and also a sports enthusiast.

When I was born, I had a large tumor in my left thigh and had to have my leg amputated at the hip when I was a year old. Because of this, my parents did not know if I would ever be able to participate in sports. At an early age, I began to show an interest in sports and chose to start with soccer. I quickly learned to adapt my style to play with my crutches and never looked back! Next I decided to give baseball a try, and thanks to some wonderful coaches, I found another sport I loved. These two sports helped me make many friends and learn to be part of a team.

The desire to try new things led me to challenge myself with flag football, where I played quarter back for two seasons. I have also started wrestling, and just this winter, I won the state championship for my age and weight. I love playing on a team and I am thankful that my parents have allowed me to go after my dreams.

I hope that when others see me play, they will be aware that a physical challenge can be overcome when you have the desire and you believe in yourself".

Chapter 24

Prayer Will Work for You

An illiterate woman who knew only two prayers-the Our Father and the Hail Mary, always carried with her a book to Church and wept copiously while she apparently read it. People who knew that she would not read, could not help but wonder.

One day out of curiosity, a saintly man asked her what she was reading and begged her to allow him to see it. The good woman told him, "You will not be able to read my book any more than I was able to read your books" But the man insisted. Therefore, she finally allowed him to see her curious books of only four pages. The first page was white and blank, "Oh", said the holy man, "There is nothing to read," "Well, answered the old woman. "On this page I read the purity of Jesus and His Blessed Mother Mary, and when I see myself so culpable, so loaded with sins I cannot help but weep". The second page was red, "On this page", she said, "I read the passion our Lord so excruciatingly on Good Friday, with His body torn and bleeding from the scourging and His head crowned with thorns". The third page was black, "Here I read", she said, "The darkness of hell with all its pains and torments". The fourth page was golden. "This page", she said, "reminds me of heaven and the resplendent glory of paradise".

Chapter 25

A Reckless Celebration Can End Up in Tragedy

A man once received the good news of a promotion in his job. He called up his wife and asked her to prepare for the evening party. He took out his car and started driving home. In addition, as he drove, he telephoned his friends, inviting them for the evening's celebration. Suddenly he saw a small crowd of people on the road. They were frantically trying to wave him to halt as a young man who had met with an accident and was lying in a pool of blood needed to be taken to hospital. But this man had no time for any charitable deed. His eyes and thoughts were focused on the party fixed for the evening. When he reached home, he received a call from somewhere saying, "Your son has met with an accident. He is in a critical condition, please, come soon". As he rushed to the hospital he saw the same people who had been thumbing a lift in order to take the young man to the hospital. He went inside. The doctor looked at him and said, "If you had brought him a little earlier he would have been saved. He is no more". It was his own son for whom he had no time to spare, perhaps thinking that it may be someone else child. In this process, he had lost his only son. The promotion, his job, his entire family life had now become meaningless to him.

It is indeed a good thing to celebrate the joyful occasions in our life. However, it should not prevent you from doing good-loving God and your neighbor.

Chapter 26

A Reckless Celebration Can End Up in Tragedy

In the year 1977, a certain airplane, with the then Prime Minister of India, Shri Moraji Desai and other VIPs on board, got caught in bad weather just when it was about to land. The pilot asked the passengers to fasten their seat belts. He and his co-pilot, both Christians, were going through severe mental agony, facing as they did, a moral dilemma. They had two options before them: they could try a nose landing or a tail landing. If a nose landing occurred, the pilots would be killed.

They were young and their families depended on them. They could not bear the thought of the loss their dear ones would suffer. How could they kill themselves? But then if the tail landing occurred, it would mean death for the VIPs. Then they remembered the threefold promise they had made when they were commissioned as pilots: they should be knowledgeable, they should be of impeccable character and in case of an emergency, they should be prepared to save others even at the cost of their own lives. The pilots overcame the struggle with their consciences and opted for the nose landing, thus saving the lives of the VIPs. Moraji Desai publicly acknowledged the sacrifice and acclaimed the heroic deeds of the pilots.

Chapter 27

Think Positive

A blind boy sat on the steps of a building with his begging bowl by his feet. He held up a sign that read: "I am blind, please help!" There were only a few coins in his bowl.

A man was walking by; he took a few coins from his pocket and dropped them into the boy's bowl. He then took the sign, turned it around, and wrote some words on it. He put the new sign back so that everyone who walked by would see the new words he had written.

Very soon, the bowl began to fill up with coins and bills. A lot more people were giving money to the blind boy. That afternoon the man who had changed the sign came to see how things were. The boy recognized his footsteps and asked; "Were you the one who changed my sign this morning? What did you write?"

The man said, "I only wrote the truth. I said what you said but I said it differently! I wrote, "Today is a beautiful day, and I cannot see it!"

Moral- Let us be thankful for what we have. Let us be creative, be innovative. Let us think differently and positively.

Chapter 28

Be an Instrument of God's Love

The world famous Paganini (1782-1840) was scheduled to begin his violin recital one evening, when he found that his Stradivarius violin had been stolen from its case and had been replaced with an old, ordinary violin. The audience was already seated and there was no time to go elsewhere and bring in another violin worthy of the maestro. Undaunted, Paganini took the old instrument, turned it to concert pitch and began to perform as if nothing untoward had happened. When he had finished his recital, the audience gave him a standing ovation. Paganini then announced, "Friends, today I've performed on an old, ordinary violin; and, I've proved to you that the music is not in the instrument but in the maestro!"

Chapter 29

We Are All Equal Before God

On a British Airways flight from Johannesburg, a middle-aged, well-off white South African woman had found herself sitting next to a black man. She called the cabin crew attendant over to complain about her seating. "What seems to be the problem madam?" asked the airhostess.

"Can't you see?" She said, "You've seated me next to a Kaffir. I cannot possibly sit next to this disgusting human. Find me another seat!" "Please calm down madam" the airhostess replied. "The flight is very full today, but I'll tell you what I'll do. I'll go and check to see if we have any seats available in club or first class". The woman cocked an arrogant look at the outraged black man beside her.

A few minutes later the airhostess returned with the good news and said to the woman, "Madam, unfortunately, as I suspected, economy is full. I've spoken to the cabin services director, and club is also full. However, we do have one seat in first class".

Before the woman had a chance to answer the airhostess continues, "It is most extraordinary to make this kind of upgrade, however, and I have had to get special permission from the captain. But, given the circumstances, the captain felt that it was outrageous that someone be forced to sit next to such an obnoxious person". With which, she turned to the black man sitting next to her, and said, "So if you'd like to get your things, sir, I have your seat ready for you in first class up at the front..."

At which point, apparently the surrounding passengers stood and gave a standing ovation while the black guy walked up to first class in the front of the plane.

Chapter 30

Why Go to Church?

A Catholic wrote a letter to the editor of a prestigious Catholic weekly and complained that it made no change in him attending Sunday Masses. "I've gone now for 30 years, and during these years I have heard about 3,000 sermons. Now I cannot remember any of them. So I think I'm wasting my time and the pastors are wasting theirs by preaching sermons".

This letter started a real controversy in the 'Letters to the editor' column, much to the delight of the editor. It went on for weeks until someone wrote the following letters: "I've been married for the last 30 years. During this period, my wife has cooked some 32,000 meals. But now I can't recall the entire menu for a single one of those meals. However, I do know this. They all nourished me and gave me the strength I needed to work. If my wife had not given me those meals, I would be physically dead today. Likewise, if I had not gone to Church for my Spiritual nourishment, I would be spiritually dead today".

Chapter 31

The Sweetest Thing Can Turn Into Bitterest

Joseph Stalin (1879-1953) was the most ruthless dictator of the former Soviet Union. He was the General Secretary of the Communist party from 1922 to 1953. In 1928, he launched a series of five-year plans for the rapid industrialization of the country and enforced collectivization of agriculture. As a result, more than 10 million farmers were killed. He ruthlessly put to death hundreds and thousands of intellectuals who opposed him .He in fact, had murdered more men and women than the maniac Hitler.

However, the surprising thing was that Stalin, as a teenager, had joined the seminary .He was expelled from there because of his revolutionary ideas- a noble desire gone awfully wrong! A man desired to save souls as a priest of God became a monster who ruthlessly mowed down people by the million.

Moral: The decay of the best is always the worst, the sweetest things turning sourest by their deeds.

Chapter 32

Remain Faithful

The Communist regime in China arrested Father Fang – Cheng for being a Christian, and tortured him to betray the names of the other Christians. One day he was produced in court for further investigation, and was shocked to see his mother in rags, chained in a corner. Obviously, she had been tortured, too.

The officer said to him, "I believe you know the Ten Commandments which your God has given you and you are supposed to obey them. Will you be kind enough to recite them for me?" Father Fang began to repeat them one by one ; when he came to the Commandment , "Honor your Father and mother," the officer stopped him and said to him, "If you really obey the commandment , you must honor your mother and save her life by revealing the names of the other Christian and their activities .

Father Fang was in a dilemma, he looked at his tortured mother and asked her, "Mother, what shall I do?" The brave mother replied, "Son, I have taught you from your childhood to love Christ and his Church. Do not worry about me. Remain faithful to the saviour and his little flock. If you betray them you will no longer be my son ".

MORAL: Faithfulness is a virtue that can take you far!

Chapter 33

Do Your Best and Leave the Rest to God

Dr. Ben Carson a member of the Seventh –Day Adventist Church, faced one of the greatest challenges of his life, viz, to separate the seven –month –old Siamese twins, joined at the skull. The surgical team practised the procedures for months because they knew that even a minute mistake could mean the difference between life and death. After fourteen hours in the operation theatre, Dr. Carson said, "We did the best we could do. The rest is up to God ".

Today Dr. Ben Carson is one of the leading pediatric neuro-surgeon in the world and his successful operation on the Siamese twins brought him into the spotlight.

Dr. Ben Carson knew that God can change people and situations, not only in a hospital but also on the streets; Born in the Detroit Gretto, Carson was accustomed to knives of a different kind. During a fight at the age of fourteen, he lunged with a knife at the stomach of another kid only to see the knife blade strike the belt buckle and break. It scared him .He realized that he needed to turn his life around. He could not do it alone. With God's help and the love and support of his mother, he came out of the streets and eventually went to Yale University. He, who used his knife to take away someone's life, now uses the knife to give life to millions.

Chapter 34

Slow and Steady Wins the Race

Shortly after the turns of the last century, a young man named Dale Carnegie, in Missouri enrolled in the state Teachers College in Warrenburg to get an education. He was a poor lad who could not afford to live in town, so he commuted three miles each day on horseback in order to attend class. He had only one good suit. His coat was too thin. He tried out for the football team and was rejected. In spite of his obvious pluck and courage, the young student was developing a deep – seated inferiority complex. His mother urged him to do something that would demonstrate his real potential, so he tried public speaking. Unfortunately, he failed at that too. At this stage in his life, everything the young man did ended in failure. Yet Dale Carnegie kept at it and eventually became the best-known teacher of public speaking in history. The lad who had failed at speaking became the personal manager of radio's celebrated newscaster and with author Lowekll Thomas developed a course of instruction on *"How to Win Friends and Influence People"* that made him a millionaire.

> "*"It does not matter how slowly you go, so long as you do not stop* ".
> - *Confucius.*"

Chapter 35

What's Love?

Love is when Mom kisses me.

Love is when Dad says, "I am proud of you my dear."

Love is when Brother says, "Hey, what do you need from my first salary?"

Love is when my Sister while doing my work says, "After my marriage who'll do your work?"

Love is when I am fed up with my studies and my friend say, "Leave it dear; we'll clear it"

Love doesn't always mean saying, "I love you? It's a feeling of love and care for someone from the heart."

Chapter 36

Hidden Rewards

Once there was a famine, a kind, rich baker sent for twenty of the poorest children in the town, and said to them, "In this basket there is a loaf for each of you. Take it, and come back to me every day at this hour till God Sends us better times."

The hungry children gathered eagerly about the basket, and most quarreled over the bread because each wished to have the largest loaf. At last they went away without even thanking the good gentleman.

But Gretchen, a poorly dressed little girl, did not quarrel or struggle with the rest, but remained standing quietly at the side. When the ill –behaved children had left, she took the smallest loaf, which alone was left in the basket, kissed the gentleman's hand, and went home.

The next day the children were as ill –behaved as before, and poor, timid Gretchen received a loaf scarcely half the one she got the first day. When she went home, and her mother cut the loaf open, many new shinning pieces of silver fell out of it.

Her mother was very much alarmed, and said, "Take the money back to the good gentleman at once, for it must have gotten into the dough by accident." But when the little girl gave the rich man her mother's message, he said, "No, my child, it was no mistake. I had the silver pieces put into the smallest loaf to reward you. Always be as contented, kind and thankful as you now are."

We never lose by giving.

Chapter 37

A Small Act of Kindness Saved a Nation

In 1982 at Stanford University, USA, an 18-years old student was struggling to pay his fees. He was an orphan and not knowing where to get money, yet he came up with a bright idea. He and a friend decided to host a musical concert on campus to raise money for their education. They reached out to the great pianist Ignacy J. Paderewski and his manager demanded a fee of $2000 for the piano recital. So, the boys began to work for the concert but unfortunately, they only sold tickets with a total collection of $1600.

They went to Paderewski and gave him the entire $1600, plus a check for the balance $400 and promised to honor the check as soonest possible. But "No", said Paderewski. He tore the check and told the two boys, "Here's the $1600. Please deduct whatever expenses you have incurred. Keep the money that you need for your fees. And just give me whatever is left." The boys were surprised and thanked him profusely. It was a small act of kindness. However, it clearly marked on them that Paderewski is a great human being. Why should he help when he did not even know them?

Paderewski later went on to become the Prime Minister of Poland. He was a great leader, but unfortunately, when the World War began, Poland was ravaged. There were more than 1.5 million people starving in his country and no money to feed them. Paderewski reached out to the US Food and Relief Administration for help. He heard there was a man call Herbert Hoover – who later became the US President.

Hoover agreed to help and quickly shipped tons of food grains to feed the starving Polish people. The calamity was averted. Paderewski was relieved and decided to go across to meet Hoover and personally thank him. When Paderewski began to thank Hoover for his noble gesture, Hoover quickly interjected and said, "You shouldn't be thanking me Mr. Prime Minister. You may not remember this, but several years ago, you helped two young students go through college. I was one of them."

We all come across situations like these in our lives. And most of us think "If I help them, what will happen to me?" But truly great people will think, "If I don't help them, what will happen to them?" and are not expecting something in return. They do it because they feel it's the right thing to do. Keep helping others for Good Karma will always return.

Chapter 38

Integrity Put To Stake

Kanyama Police officer walks into butchery in Makeni, just before closing time and ask, "Do you still have chicken?" The butcher opens his deep freezer, takes out the only chicken left, and puts it on the scale. It weights 1.5 kg. The officer looks at the chicken and the scale, then asks, "Do you have one that's a bit bigger than this one?"

The butcher puts the chicken back into the freezer and then takes it out again. This time, he craftily keeps his thumb on the scale pan, making it show 2 kg. "That's wonderful", says the police officer. I'll take both chickens, please!"

In a situation like this, you realize that your integrity and your reputation are on the line. Your wisdom becomes foolishness, and your cunning ways become stupidity.

Remember : Always tell the truth and you will be free! A good name is better than riches. Live to express yourself truthfully, not to impress others.

Chapter 39

The Unseen Tears

A fifteen year old mother was going with her two year old son to Church and suddenly they passed a group of boys who started sending words to her : "Hey you bitch, you slut, a sex pervert . Why didn't you wait to have sex, ha ha ha ! You were thirsty for it, imagine at that age with this son?"

They spoke a lot of words to her but she kept quiet, then one boy from the back said: "What are you going to do in the Church, you prostitute? May be you want to sleep with the pastor".

Then the young lady turned to them gently and said in a calm voice: "Who are you to blame me for my sins? Are you sure you are clean in God's eyes? Pray that what happened to me doesn't happen to any of your sisters or someone you love".

After saying that, tears started running down her face. But the boys laughed and said more words to her. She continued and went to Church.

As she passed, a man came and found the boys still talking and laughing at her, and said to them, "Do you know her?" They said, "No."

He said to them; "This girl, when she was twelve and half years, a group of man attacked their home. They killed her father and her Mum, they robbed all the things that they had in the house and as they were about to leave, one of them saw her hiding in the corner and they all raped her. So she doesn't know the father of her child and she has nowhere to stay."

The boy's hearts were filled with pity, and they regretted all they had said, they felt as if they should do all it takes to help her.

MORAL - Before you accuse someone, first understand the cause and why he/she did that thing. When you are pointing one finger to someone, know that there are other three fingers pointing at you. Let us not accuse each other but help each other.

Chapter 40

Dear Dad, Where You Stand?

Son: "Daddy , may I ask you a question .? "
Dad: "Yeah sure , what is it ? "
Son: "Daddy , how much do you make an hour ? "
Dad: "That's none of your business. Why do you ask such a thing? "
Son: "I just want to know. Please tell me how much do you make an hour? "
Dad: "If you must know , I make $100 an hour ".
Son: "Oh! (With his head down). Daddy may I please borrow $50? "
The Dad was furious.
Dad: "If the only reason you asked that is so you can borrow some money to buy a silly toy or some other nonsense , now you march yourself straight to your room and go to bed . Think about why you are being so selfish. I work hard every day for such childish behavior".

The little boy quietly went to his room and shut the door. The man sat down and started to get even angrier about the little boy's questions. How dare he ask such questions only to get some money?

After about an hour or so, the man had calmed down, and started to think: May be there was something he really needed to buy with that $50 and he really did not ask for money very often. The man went to the door of the little boy's room and opened the door.
Dad: "Are you asleep, son?"
Son: "No Daddy, I'm awake "
Dad: "I've been thinking maybe I was too hard on you earlier. It has been a long day and I took out my aggravation on you. Here is the $ 50 you asked for "
The little boy sat straight up smiling.
Son: "Oh, Thank you Daddy!"
Then, reaching under his pillow he pulled out some crumpled up bills. The man saw that the boy already had money, started to get angry again. The little boy slowly counted out his money, and then looked up at his father.

Dad: "Why do you want more money if you already have some?"
Son: "Because I didn't have enough, but now I do. Daddy, I have $ 100 now. Can I buy an hour of your time? Please come home early tomorrow. I would like to have dinner with you ".

The father was crushed. He put his arms around his little son, and he begged for his forgiveness.

It is just a short reminder to all of you working so hard in life. We should not let time slip through our fingers without having spent some time with those who really matter to us, those close to our hearts. Do remember to share that $100 worth of your time with someone you love? If we die tomorrow, the company that we are working for could easily replace us in a matter of days. However, the family and friends we leave behind will feel the loss for the rest of their lives. In addition, come to think of it, we pour ourselves more into work than into our family.

Chapter 41

Always an Attitude of Gratitude

A king had a male servant who, in all circumstances always said to him, "My king, do not be discouraged because everything God does is perfect, no mistakes.

One day, they went hunting and a wild animal attacked the king, the servant managed to kill the animal but couldn't prevent his majesty from losing a finger. Furious and without showing gratitude, the king said; "If God was good, I would not have been attacked and lost one finger."

The servant replied; despite all these things, I can only tell you that God is good and everything he does is perfect, He is never wrong. Outraged by the response, the king ordered the arrest of his servant. Later, he left for another hound and was captured by savages who use human beings for sacrifice.

In the altar, the savages found out that the king did not have one finger in place; he was released because he was considered not "complete" to be offered to gods.

On his return to the palace, he authorized the release of his servant and said; "My friend, God was really good to me. I was almost killed but for lack of a single finger, I was let go."

But I have a question; "If God is so good, why did he allow me to put you in jail?" He replied; "My king, if I had gone with you, I would have been sacrificed because I have no missing finger."

Everything God does is perfect, he is never wrong. Often we complain about life, and the negative things that happen to us, forgetting that nothing is random and that everything has a purpose.

Chapter 42

Do Not Boast on God's Mercy

An atheist wanted to tease those who observe Sabbath on Sunday. He had prepared his land for cultivation on Sunday. On another Sunday, he sows seeds. Manuring and all the works for the field had been on Sundays. He had a very good crops. The next day he had made an advertisement in the newspaper, stating, "I had all my works done on Sundays, breaking the Sabbath. But on harvest I had better crops than you, my friend who observe Sabbath'. He received a beautiful reply, "My friend, it is your misunderstanding that God punishes those who do not observe Sabbath, at the time of reaping. Harvest and good crops are not the criteria of God's blessing. Who knows how much you have lost in between. How many blessings have gone out of your way during this time? Do not boast on God's mercy"

Chapter 43

Special Consideration for the Atheist

Phillip Brooks, a zealous missionary, was on his deathbed battling against sickness in the hospital. Many renowned visitors came to see him. But nobody was allowed to get in.

At the same time the news of the arrival of the guests' were informed to him. As the time passed by, there came a well-known atheist who was a friend of Brooks. As the news reached Brooks, he told the doctor to allow him to come in. Everyone was surprised, even Bishops were waiting outside! Atheist had his head little up and walked inside.

Brooks said in a trembling voice, "All those outside are really great people, I know. However, possibly I could see them in the other world too but about you, I am afraid, whether I will meet you again. So I called you in".

It is said that these words led the atheist to conversion.

Chapter 44

More Economic Business

A Christian businessman was engaged in business all the days including Sunday. His wife and children approached the Parish priest and requested him to correct this practice. The parish priest approached the man and said, "Is it not improper that you work on Sundays, as a Christian?" He was intelligent. 'Dear Father, do you think that I oppose you. On all days, I have business trials. One or the other problems will have to be solved. Even Jesus was of the opinion that, "if your goat or ox falls into a well on a Sunday, you must take it out", I think.

The priest thought for a moment and said, "Yes, my dear child, Jesus had said that, but I think if that goat or ox have the tendency to fall into the well on all Sundays, it is better either to sell the goat or fill the well properly. Otherwise you will have heavy economic losses. The business man was silent.

Chapter 45

The Great Business Done

John Vanamaker was a great businessman. He had crores of rupees as capital assets. On the zenith of fame and power, there was an interview conducted. The interviewer asked, "What was the greatest business done by you. You took so much pain but regretted never?"

All we were expecting great business adventure from him. However, he said, 'when I was eight, I had the desire to get a beautifully binded book which was in the hands of my class teacher. It was costly. So I had to work day and night. I saved so very hard that many times I thought I would not make it. But I did. After I bought it, I never regretted on it. Because it was the Bible, which guided me all these years".

Chapter 46

Someone Above

A man had gone to a corn field to steal. His four-year-old child accompanied him. The man looked around at every nook and corner and started collecting corns into a sack. Suddenly the boy asked very innocently, "Dad, you had looked all around, but you did not look above. There can be someone watching us". He repented and went home without stealing. The child taught him a great lesson in life and changed his life forever. He was never the same father and husband anymore.

Chapter 47

Do not Complain

A man wanted to become a monk so he went to the monastery and talked to the head monk. The head monk said, "You must take a vow of silence and can only say two words every three years". The man agreed and after the first three years, the head monk came to him and said, "What are your two words?"

"Food cold!" the man replied.

Three more years went by and the head monk came to him and said, "What are your two words?"

"Robe dirty!" the man exclaimed.

Three more years went by and the head monk came to him and said, "What are your two word?"

"I quit", said the man.

"Well", the head monk replied, "I am not surprised. You have done nothing but complain ever since you got here!"

Complaining about everything in our lives will slowly ruin us.

Chapter 48

A Mother's Heart

A six year old boy asks his Mom, "Mom, what are you going to get me for my 18th birthday?" The Mother answers, "Son that's still a long way".

The boy turns seventeen and one day he faints. His Mom takes him to the hospital and the doctor says, "Madam your child has a bad heart". The child being seated on the stretcher asks his Mom, "Did he tell you I'm going to die?" The Mom started crying.

The boy finally recovers on his 18th birthday, he comes home and on his bed was a letter his Mom had left him. The letter said, "Son if you are reading this it's because everything went well. Remember that day, you asked me what was I giving you on your 18th birthday and I didn't know what to answer you?"

"I gave you my heart, take care of it and Happy Birthday son".

Nothing is bigger than Mom's heart.

Chapter 49

My One Eyed Mother

My Mom had only one eye. I hated her… she was such an embarrassment. She cooked for students and teachers to support the family. There was this one day during elementary school where my Mom came to say hello to me. I was so embarrassed. How could she do this to me? I ignored, threw her a hateful look and ran out. The next day at school one of my classmates said, "EEEEE, Your Mom only has one eye!"

I wanted to bury myself. I also wanted my Mom to just disappear. I confronted that day and said, "If you are only going to make me a laughing stock, why don't you just die?" My Mom did not respond… I did not even stop to think for a second about what I had said, because I was full of anger. I was oblivious to her feelings.

I wanted her out of that house, and have nothing to do with her. So I studied really hard and got a chance to go abroad to study. Then I got married. I bought a house of my own. I had kids and was happy with my life, my kids and the comforts. Then one day my mother came to visit me. She hadn't seen me in years and she didn't even meet her grandchildren.

When she stood by the door, my children laughed at her, and I yelled at her for coming over uninvited. I screamed at her, "How dare you come to my house and scare my children! Get out of here now". And to this, my mother quietly answered, "Oh, I'm so sorry, I may have gotten the wrong address and she disappeared out of sight".

One day, a letter regarding a school reunion came to my house. So I lied to my wife that I was going on a business trip. After the union, I went to the old shack just out of curiosity. My neighbour said that she died. I did not shed a single tear they handed me a letter that she had wanted me to have:

"My dearest son, I think of you all the time. I'm sorry that I came to your house and scared your children. I was so glad when I heard you were coming for the reunion. But I may not be able to even get out of bed to see you. I'm sorry that I was a constant embarrassment to you when you were growing up. You see…when you were very little, you got into an accident, and lost your eye. As a mother, I couldn't stand watching you having to grow up with one eye. So I gave you mine. I was so proud of my son who was seeing a whole new world for me, in my place, with that eye. With all my love to you,

Your Mother".

Always love your parents. They are a blessing to you.

Chapter 50

That's Your Profit

A small town businessman had very simple ways of keeping his accounts. His son, a qualified accountant criticized his father's unconventional old-fashioned method. "How can you run your business, and know what your profits are?" he enquired. "Son", replied the businessman. "When I got off the boat I had only the pants I was wearing. Today, your sister is a teacher, your brother is a Doctor, and you are an accountant. I have a car, a home and a business. Everything is paid for. You add it all up and subtract the pants. That's your profit!"

Dear friends, never underestimate your parent's wisdom.

Chapter 51

Power of Words

A group of frogs was travelling through the woods, and two of them fell into a deep pit. When the other frogs saw how deep the pit was, they told the two frogs that they were as good as dead. The two frogs ignored the comments and tried to jump out of the pit with all their might. The other frogs kept telling them to stop, and they were as good as dead. Finally, one of the frogs took heed to what the other frogs were saying and gave up. He fell down and died. The other frog continued to jump as hard as he could. Once again, the crowd of frogs yelled at him to stop the pain and just die. He jumped even harder and finally made it out. When he got out, the other frogs said, "Did you not hear us?" the frog explained to them that he was partially deaf. He thought they were encouraging him the entire time.

This story teaches us two lessons:

1. There is power of life and death in the tongue. An encouraging words to someone who is down can lift them up and help them make it through the day.
2. A destructive word to someone who is down can be what it takes to kill them. Be careful of what you say. Speak life to those who cross your path. The power of words… it is sometimes hard to understand that an encouraging word can go such a long way. Anyone can speak words that tend to rob another of the spirit to continue in difficult times. Special is the individual who will take the time to encourage another.

Chapter 52

Before You Speak of Someone

In ancient Greece, Socrates was reputed to hold knowledge in high esteem. One day an acquaintance met the great philosophers and said, "Do you know what I just heard about your friend?"

"Hold on a minute," Socrates replied, "Before you talk to me about my friend, it might be good idea to take a moment and filter what you're going to say. That's what I call it the triple filter test. The first filter is truth. Have you made absolutely sure that what you are about to tell me is true?"

"Well, no", the man said, "actually I just heard about it and…", "All right," said Socrates. "So you don't really know if it's true or not. Now, let's try the second filter, the filter of goodness. Is what you are about to tell me about my friend something good?"

"Umm, no, on the contrary…" "So," Socrates continued, "You want to tell me something bad about my friend, but you're not certain it's true. You may still pass the test though, because there's one filter left- the filter of usefulness. Is what you want to tell me about my friend going to be useful to me?" "No, not really", "Well" concluded Socrates, "if what you want to tell me is neither true, nor good, nor even useful, why tell it to me at all?"

Chapter 53

Weakness Can Be Strength

A ten year old boy decided to study judo despite the fact that he had lost his left arm in a devastating car accident. The boy began lessons with an old Japanese Judo master. The boy was doing well, so he couldn't understand why, after three months of training the master had taught him only one move. "Sensei", (Teacher in Japanese) the boy finally said, shouldn't I be learning more moves?" "This is the only move you know, but this is the only move you'll ever need to know", the sensei replied. Not quite understanding, but believing in his teacher the boy kept training.

Several months later, the sensei took the boy to his first tournament. Surprising himself, the boy easily won his first two matches. The third match proved to be more difficult, but after sometime, his opponent became impatient and charged, the boy deftly used his one move to win the match. Still amazed by his success the boy was now in the finals. Then this time his opponent was bigger, stronger and more experienced. For a while, the boy appeared to be overmatched. Concerned that the boy might get hurt, the referee called a timeout. He was about to stop the match when the sensei intervened. "No", the sensei insisted, "Let him continue". Soon after the match resumed, his opponent made a critical mistake: he dropped his guard. Instantly the boy used his move to pin him. The boy had won the match and the tournament. He was the champion. On the way home, the boy and sensei reviewed every move in each and every match. The boy summoned the courage to ask what was really on his mind.

"Sensei, how did I win the tournament with only one move?"

"You won for two reasons," the sensei answered." "First, you've almost mastered one of the most difficult throw in all of judo. And second, the only known defence for that move is for your opponent to grab your left arm". The boy's biggest weakness had become his biggest strength.

Chapter 54

Never Underestimate Anyone

A young boy enters a barber shop and the barber whispers to his customers, "This is the dumbest kid in the world. Watch while I prove it to you". The barber puts a five rupee coin in one hand and two one rupee coins (1+1=2) in the other, then calls the boy over and asks, "Which do you want, son?" The boy takes the two one-rupee coins and leaves. "What did I tell you?" said the barber. "That kid never learns!" Later, when the customer leaves, he sees the same young boy coming out of the ice cream store. "Hey son! May I ask you a question? Why did you take two one rupee coins instead of five rupee coins?" The boy licked his cone and replied, "Because the day I take the five rupee coin, the game is over".

Chapter 55

We Understand People as We Are

There is a legend about a wise man who was sitting outside his village. A traveler came up and asked him, "What kind of people live in this village, because I am looking to move from my present one!" The wise man asked, "What kind of people lives where you want to move from?" The man said, "They are mean, cruel, and rude". The wise man replied, "The same kind of people lives in this village too". After sometime, another traveler came by and asked the same question and the wise man asked him, "What kind of people live where you want to move from?" And the traveler replied, "The people are very kind, courteous, polite and good." The wise man said, "You will find the same kind of people here too."

Chapter 56

What Costs Some Knowledge?

A giant ship engine failed. The ship's owners tried one expert after another, but none of them could figure out how to fix the engine. Then they brought in an old man who had been fixing ships since he was a young man. He carried a large bag of tools with him, and when he arrived, he immediately went to work. He inspected the engine very carefully, top to bottom. Two of the ship's owners were there, watching this man, hoping he would know what to do. After looking things over, the old man reached into his bag and pulled out a small hammer. He gently tapped something. Instantly, the engine lurched into life. He carefully put his hammer away. The engine was fixed! A week later, the owner received a bill from the old man for ten thousand dollars. "What?!" the owner exclaimed. "He hardly did anything!" So they wrote the old man a note saying, "Please send us an itemized bill".

The man sent a bill that read:

Tapping with a hammer… $2.00

Knowing where to tap… $9,998.00

Effort is important, but knowing where to make an effort makes all the difference! Keep studying hard. Don't give up!

Chapter 57

Leave Your Troubles Outside

The carpenter I hired to help me restore an old farmhouse had just finished a rough first day on the job. A flat tire made him lose an hour of work, his electric saw quit, and now his ancient pick truck refused to start, while I drove him home, he invited me in to meet the family.

As we walked towards the front door, he paused briefly at a small tree, touching the tips of the branches with both hands.

After opening the door, he underwent an amazing transformation. His face was wreathed in smiles, and he hugged his two small children and then gave his wife a kiss. Afterwards, he walked me to my car. We passed the tree, and my curiosity got the better of me. I asked him about what I had seen him do earlier. "Oh, that's my trouble tree", he replied. "I know I can't help having troubles on the job, but one thing for sure, troubles don't belong in the house with my wife and children. So I just hang them up one the tree every night when I come home. Then in the morning, I pick them up again". "Funny thing is ", he smiled, "When I come out in the morning to pick them up, there aren't nearly as many as I remember hanging up the night before".

Chapter 58

You Never Know Who is Watching Your Actions

Several years ago a young priest moved to London. He often took the bus from his home to the down town area. Some weeks after he arrived, he had occasion to ride a bus. When he sat down he discovered that the driver had accidentally given him twenty pence too much change. As he considered what to do, he thought to himself, "You better give the twenty pence back. It would be wrong to keep it".

Then he thought, "Oh forget it, it's only twenty pence". Who would worry about this little amount? Anyway, the bus company already gets too much fare; they will never miss it. Accept it as a gift from the Almighty, and keep quiet".

When his stop came, the priest paused momentarily at the door, then he handed the twenty pence back to the driver and said: "Here, you gave me too much change".

The driver with a smile replied; "Aren't you the new parish priest in this area? I have been thinking lately about going to worship at your Church. I just wanted to see what you would do if I gave you too much change".

When the young priest stepped off the bus, his knees became weak and soft. He had to grab the nearest light pole, held for support, and look up to the heavens, and cried:

"Oh my Jesus, I almost sold your Christianity for twenty pence!"

We may never see what impact our actions have on people... Sometimes we are the only "Bible" someone will ever read, or the only Christianity someone will see. What we need to provide is an example for others to see. Be careful of how you behave, and be honest always: you never know who is watching your actions.

Chapter 59

Alexander the Great's Last Three Wishes

Alexander, after conquering many kingdoms, was returning home. On the way, he fell ill and it took him to his death bed. With death staring him in his face, Alexander realised how much his conquest, his great army, his sharp sword and all his wealth were of no use.

He now longed to reach home to see his mother's face and bid her adieu. But, he had to accept the fact that his sinking health would not permit him to reach his distant homeland. So, the mighty conqueror lay prostrate and pale, helplessly waiting to breathe his last. He calls his generals and said, "I will depart from this world soon, I have three wishes, please carry them out without fail". With tears flowing down their cheeks, the generals agreed to abide by their king's last wishes".

"My first desire is that," said Alexander. "My Physicians alone must carry my coffin". After a pause, he continued, "Secondly, I desire that when my coffin is being carried to the grave, the path leading to the graveyard be strewn with gold, silver and precious stones which I have collected in my treasury". The king felt exhausted after saying this. He took a minute's rest and continued. My third and last wish is that both my hands be kept dangling out of my coffin". The people who had gathered there wondered at the King's strange wishes. But no one dared bring the question to their lips. Alexander's favourite general kissed his hand and pressed them to his heart. "O king, we assure you that all your wishes will be fulfilled. But tell us why do you make such strange wishes?" At this Alexander took a deep breath and said: "I would like the world to know of the three lessons I have just learnt. I want my Physicians to carry my coffin because people would realise that no doctor on this earth can really cure anybody. They are powerless and cannot save a person from the clutches of death. So let not people take life for granted. The second wish is strewing gold, silver and other riches on the path of the graveyard is to tell people that not even a fraction of gold will come with me. I will spent all my life with the greed for power, earning riches but cannot take anything with me. Let people realise that it is a sheer waste of time to chase wealth.

And about my third wish of having my hands dangling out of the coffin, I wish my people to know that I came empty handed into this world and empty handed I go out of this world". With these words, the King closed his eyes. Soon he let death conquer him and he breathed his last.

Chapter 60

Hunt for the Mule

Ignatius of Loyola was riding on a mule. He was heading towards a port city in Spain in the hope of going to Jerusalem. On the way he met a Moor (A Moor is a Muslim from Northern Africa). The Moor presented his arguments against the virginity of Mary after the birth of Christ. Ignatius, who was still a Knight, did not have enough knowledge to argue back. The Moor hurried and went ahead of Ignatius. Ignatius was indignant and angry at the audacity of the Moor in insulting our lady, and he decided to give the Moor a taste of his sword. However, Ignatius could not make up his mind. So he prayed, "Let the mule take the road of destiny". If the mule followed the King's highway, then it will take Ignatius to the Moor. If on the other hand, the mule took the narrow road, then Ignatius will go to the port city. Surprisingly, the mule took the narrow road, and Ignatius went to Jerusalem. If, Ignatius took the King's highway to pursue the Moor, the Catholic Church would have probably lost a great saint and no Jesuit Universities would have ever existed.

We will come to the crossroads many times in our life. We do not know the right decision to make. We should pray and allow the mule of providence to take us to our destiny. The path will be narrow and the road will be tough to travel but God will guide us to our destiny. When not sure, visit the Lord, stay in his presence and pray fervently to lead you to your destiny. God will hear your genuine prayer. He keeps his word. He is trust worthy. He is dependable and real. If you are destined to be a saint, the distractions of the Moor will not stop you.

Chapter 61

The Young Diver

A young man who had been raised as an atheist was training to be an Olympic diver. The only religious influence in his life came from his outspoken Christian friend. The young diver never really paid much attention to his friend's sermons, but he heard them often. One night the diver went to the indoor pool at the college he attended.

The lights were all off, but as the pool had big skylights and the moon was bright, there was plenty of light to practice by. The young man climbed up to the highest diving boards and as he turned his back to the pool on the edge of the board and extended his arm out, he saw his shadow on the wall. The shadow of his body was in the shape of a cross. The man felt a strange feeling, like someone was speaking to him. Instead of diving, he knelt down and finally asked God to come into his life. As the young man stood, a maintenance man walked in and turned the lights on. The pool had been drained for repairs.

Jesus will never be late to save you. The cross is our only means of redemption. Jesus died on the cross for you and me. Whether we take it seriously or not, He will make it clear to you one day.

Chapter 62

To Sleep Peacefully

A boy and a girl were playing together; the boy had a collection of marbles. The girl had some sweets with her. The boy told the girl that he will give her all his marbles in exchange for her sweets. The girl agreed.

The boy kept the biggest and the most beautiful marble aside and gave the rest to the girl. The girl gave him all her sweets as she had promised.

That night, the girl slept peacefully. But the boy couldn't sleep as he kept wondering if the girl had hidden some sweets from him the way he had hidden his best marbles.

You think in the way you act. If you don't give your hundred percent in a relationship, you'll always keep doubting if the other person has given his or her hundred percent. This is applicable for any relationship (viz. love, friendship, employer-employee etc.) give your hundred percent to everything you do and sleep peacefully.

Chapter 63

Two Wolves

One evening an old man told his grandson about a battle that goes on inside people. He said' "my son, the battle is between two wolves inside us all.

"One is Evil – it is anger, envy, jealousy, sorrow, regret, greed, arrogance, self pity, guilt, resentment, inferiority, lies, false pride, superiority and ego.

"The other is good – it is joy, peace, love, hope, serenity, humility, kindness, benevolence, empathy, generosity, truth, compassion and faith."

The grandson thought about it for a minute and then asked his grandfather: "Which wolf wins?"

The old man simply replied, "The one you feed."

Chapter 64

Providence of God Never Fails

Many years ago in a small Indian village, a farmer had the misfortune of owning a large sum of money to a female village moneylender. The female moneylender, who was old, fat and ugly, fancied the farmer's handsome son, Cliff.

Therefore, she proposed a bargain.

She said she would forgive the farmer's debt if she could marry his son. Both the farmer and his son were horrified by the proposal.

So the cunning female moneylender suggested that they let providence decide the matter. She told them that she would put a black pebble and a white pebble into an empty money bag. Then the son would have to pick one pebble from the bag.

If he picked the black pebble, he would become her husband and the father's debt would be forgiven.

If he picked the white pebble he need not marry her and the father's debt would still be forgiven.

But if he refused to pick a pebble, his father would be thrown into jail.

They were standing on a pebble-strewn path in the farmer's field. As they talked, the moneylender bent over to pick up two pebbles. As she picked them up, the sharp-eyed son noticed that she had picked up two black pebbles and put them into the bag. She then told the son to close his eyes and picked one pebble from the moneybag.

Now, if he reveals the dishonesty of the lady, it would be harmful for his father. He also thought that providence of God would lead him to a better conclusion that can overcome the dilemma.

The son put his hand into the moneybag and drew out a pebble. Without looking at it, he fumbled and let it fall onto the pebble-strewn path where it immediately became lost among all the other pebbles.

"Oh, how clumsy of me," he said. 'But never mind, if you look into the bag for the one that is left, you will be able to tell which pebble I picked.

Since the remaining pebble is black, it must be assumed that he had picked the white one. And since the moneylender dared not admit her dishonesty, the son changed what seemed an impossible situation into an extremely advantageous one.

Chapter 65

Following the King

A king had built a palace on the top of a mountain. When the palace was ready, the king placed all his gold jewels and precious stones into some boxes, which his servants loaded on camels. They started for the palace. But as they were climbing the mountain one of the camel stumbled against a stone and fell down. The box that the camel was carrying dropped to the ground and broke. Hundreds of precious stones were scattered about and rolled along the path. "Keep for yourself all that you can gather," the king declared with a broad gesture to his servants. And the king went on his way along while his people had stopped to fill their pockets with the precious stones. But the king heard some footsteps behind him. He turned around and saw his little servant boy. What are you doing here? Why did you not go and collect the precious stones? The boy looked at the master and simply replied, "I am following the king."

Following Christ means, no turning back. It means self-surrender and total commitment. Are we ready to leave everything? There is a risk in following the master, because we may lose even what we have, but are we ready for it?

Chapter 66

Honesty Makes Character

In March 1961, in the city of Los Angeles, a truck was carrying a large amount of money from the bank and a canvas bag containing $240,000 fell out of the truck unobserved by the guards, it was picked up by a man called Douglas Johnson, aged 50, an unemployed Negro window cleaner. He had been out of work for three months. He took the money and gave it to the police. When he was asked his answer was, "I thought if I kept that money, I would never be able to look at my three kids in the face again. I teach my children to trust God and be honest and if I don't do that how can I face my kids?"

Chapter 67

To Serve, Not To Be Served

In the American Revolutionary War, during preparation for a battle, a man in civilian clothes passed a corporal who was arrogantly ordering his men to lift a heavy beam. The man stopped and asked the corporal, "Why don't you help them?" "Sir", the answer came back indignantly, "I am the corporal." With a muttered apology, the stranger stripped off his coat and pitched in to help the soldiers. Mr. Corporal, he said, when the task was done, whenever you haven't enough men to do a job, call on your Commander-in-Chief. I will be glad to help, with that, George Washington put on his coat and left.

A good leader is a good shepherd. He gives his life in service. He gives whole-heartedly without expecting anything in return.

Chapter 68

For the Love of Others

Some years ago there was a terrible wreck on Park Avenue in New York City, involving train. Among the victims was a young man named Peter Murphy. The engine had pinned down his feet and legs. With great effort he worked one leg free and was just about to get the other loose when the roof of a coach fell down on both legs. As he writhed in agony, Chief Farrell of the fire department came to him. Murphy begged to have the timbers lifted from his legs. "If I do that, said Farrell, the roof will fall on the other side, where there are women and children." "I didn't think of that," said Murphy. "Let it stay, then. I'll stand the pain." For another pain-filled half an hour Murphy stayed there, until the victims had been removed from danger. At last he was dragged out and taken to a hospital. When released from the hospital two months later, two thousand people walked as escorts to take him home.

Chapter 69

Care for Others

One day a boy went to an ice-cream shop and asked the waitress, how much is an ice-cream cone? She said, seventy-five cents. The boy started counting the coins he had in his hand. Then he asked "How much was a small cup of ice-cream?" The waitress impatiently replied, "Sixty five Cents. The boy said, "I will have the small cup." He had his ice cream, paid the bill and left. When the waitress came to pick up the empty plate, she was touched, underneath were ten one-cent coins as tips. The little boy had consideration for the waitress before he ordered his ice-cream. He showed his sensitivity and caring. He thought of others before himself.

Chapter 70

Brotherly Love

There were two brothers, one was a bachelor and another was a married man. They owned a farm and they worked together in cultivation. That year they got an abundance of grain. One half of the grain went to one brother and the other half to the other. Everything went on well. But the married woke from sleep and started to think. This is not fair. My brother is not married and he gets only half of the produce of the farm. I am with my wife and children and I have all the security I need for my old age. But who will care for my brother when he grows old? He needs to save for his old age and his need is greater than mine. With this thought, he got out of his bed, took a sack full of grain and poured into his brother's granary.

The bachelor brother too began to think in his sleep and say to himself, this is not fair. My brother has a wife and three kids and he gets only half the measure. I have no one except myself to support. I need only a little to survive. My brother's need is obviously greater than mine. He needs more than I. So he got out of bed and poured a sack full of grain into his brother's granary. What a way to love each other!

Chapter 71

Loving till Death

A Christian group was going around surveying homes in Sussex in England. They came to a house and after some initial questions, they asked the lady of the house, "When did you marry and what does your husband do?" I was married 22 years ago and for the last 20 years after our marriage, my husband remained at home loving me", the wife replied. They were a bit confused until, totally paralyzed and practically motionless on his bed. The group curiously asked how she lived 20 years with a paralyzed husband. She replied, "When I married him 22 years ago, before the altar, I knew that I was marrying the person not the body. It does not matter to me what his or my physical state is.

All I know is that I can love him still and he can love me still". Then she pointed out a wall plaque on the wall opposite her husband's bed that read, "For better or for worse, I will love you, till death do us apart."

Chapter 72

Change of Heart

Christians in Romania were persecuted many years ago under Communist rule. They were tortured very badly. One day it so happened that a Communist police officer was thrown into a cell full of Christians. Surprised at this a Christian asked the officer how he came to be a fellow prisoner among those he had persecuted. In tears the police officer said "One day as I sat in my office, a boy entered with a flower in his hand. He told me his name and explained, "Captain, you are the one who arrested my mother. Today is her birthday. I always use to bring her a flower on this day. I can't do so this time because of you, so I decided to bring flower to your wife and tell her of my love. My own mother is a Christian who taught us to love our enemies, to reward evil with good." After that I was no longer any good as a Communist Police Officer. That's why they threw me in with you."

Chapter 73

Religion Without God

A man was given a transfer from one town to another. He went looking for a temple and found one at the street corner. But the priest somehow found out that the man belonged to a different caste. Being a prejudiced person, he tactfully tried to discourage the man from entering the temple. The man could sense that he was not welcomed. To soften the blow, the priest tried to dissuade him, saying, "Go back tonight, and talk to God. And see what he says to you". The man left. The next day he came to the temple again. This time the priest asked him, "Did you speak to God last night?" The man replied, "Of course". The priest asked, "So, what did God say?" The man answered, "God told me, 'Don't even try to enter that temple. Since the time, they built it 35 years ago they haven't allowed me to enter the temple. How do you think they are going to allow you?"

Worship should bring people together and not divide them. A God who hates the neighbor cannot be a true God. In the same way a religion that creates enmity cannot be a true religion. It is not worth following.

Chapter 74

Why Should I ask God?

Arthur Ashe, the legendary Afro-American Wimbledon player was dying of cancer. He received letters from his fans, worldwide, one of which read: "Why did God select you for such a dreadful disease?" Ashe replied, "The world over, 5 crore children start playing tennis, only 5 lakh turn professional, 5,000 come to grand slams, only 50 reach Wimbledon, four to the semifinals and two to the finals. When I won the Wimbledon crown, I never asked God "Why me?" Today, in pain, I shouldn't be asking God, 'Why me?' Wimbledon crowns, Cancer cross. That is Christianity.

Chapter 75

Don't Sell Your Conscience

Abraham Lincoln was a very successful practicing Lawyer, once someone asked him to take up a case. After hearing the detail Lincoln said, "I understand your case. It is technically strong but ethically weak. I cannot accept it. Because while I am arguing it, at the back of my mind all the time, I will keep saying to myself, "Lincoln, you are a liar. Lincoln you are a liar. I will not be able to live with myself."

Chapter 76

To Jesus Through Mary

A mother is taking her paralytic ten-year-old son to Lourdes, and tells him on the way that anything asked of Jesus through his mother is never denied. They arrived in Lourdes and attended the blessing of the sick with the Most Blessed Sacrament. When the priest passes by and gives his blessing, the child says to Jesus, 'If you don't cure me I will tell your Mother". The priest is moved by these words, and comes back to the child and blesses him again. The child once more cries out to Jesus, 'If you don't cure me, I will tell your Mother". The child was cured instantly. It was a Miracle.

Chapter 77

Start Mornings Right

A Man once took his fine Swiss watch to a jeweler for adjustment. The jeweler asked, "When do you wind your watch?" "Why, at night, before I retire", replied the man. "Oh", said the jeweler, "a watch as fine as that should be wound in the morning, so that it can start the day on a strong spring. It would then be prepared against the bumps and shocks of the day.

What is good for the watch is good for the human spirit. We should start our days and our careers on a strong spring-God.

Chapter 78

The Bliss of Married Life

A youngster was thinking of getting married. So he wrote to his father for some personal advice. His father wrote back:

I can't tell how happy I am to hear about your intention to get married. You will find marriage the most wonderful state of bliss and happiness. As I look across the table at your dear mother, I realize with great pride how full and wonderful our years together have been. By all means, get married. You have our blessings. It will be the happiest day of your life. Sincerely Dad….

Then he wrote something in the post script.

P.S.: Your mother just left the room. Stay single, you idiot!

Marriage is like a fortress. People who are inside are trying to come out and those outside are interested in getting in!

Chapter 79

The Inveterate Gambler

A not-so good looking gambler walked up to a construction site and approached the foreman. 'Good morning Sir, I am Vinay. Have you got a job for me?"

The foreman said, "Sure thing, be here tomorrow at eight o'clock sharp."

Next day a Mercedes pulled up and out stepped a Chauffeur who opened the door for Vinay. The stunned foreman was curious and asked Vinay if the Mercedes was his. "Yes", said Vinay. "It's mine alright".

"Well, you see, I'm a professional gambler. I gamble on anything, anytime. For instance, I'll bet you hundred rupees that you have a big mole on the right thigh", asserted Vinay.

The foreman was quite sure that there was no mole on his right thigh, accepted the offer and proceeded to pull down his pant to show him. But Vinay complained about the light and asked the foreman to move over the door where he had a good look and saw that there was no mole in sight, and paid the hundred rupees.

"You lost", laughed the foreman, putting the money in his pocket. "I thought you were a professional gambler".

"I am", said Vinay and continued "See the fifteen construction worker standing on those balconies? I bet them all two hundred rupees each that I'd have you remove your pant in broad day light near the door before lunch!" said Vinay.

Moral: Never underestimate anyone from his appearance.

Chapter 80

Blessing in Disguise

An illiterate man in Bangalore applied for a job as attendant at a public toilet. When it was found that he could not write his name, he was denied the job. He managed to borrow some amount and went into the business of vegetable selling. In course of time he expanded his business until he owned a chain of stores and became wealthy. One day, instead of signing his name at the bank, he gave his thumb impression. The bank manager, after excusing himself said, "You have done so well with no education, what would you have done if you'd had the advantage of schooling?"

The man replied "Oh! If I had been educated, I'd have been a public toilet attendant".

Chapter 81

Use Your Creativity

A certain doctor had travelled over a kilometer in a taxi when he suddenly discovered he had no money with him. He tapped the window and told the driver, "Stop at this petty shop for a while. I dropped a five hundred note in the taxi. Since it is too dark, I need a matchstick to locate it".

When the doctor emerged from the petty shop, he encountered a pleasant sight. There was no taxi in sight!

Chapter 82

Inspiration: A Doctor's Wisdom

A worried woman went to her gynecologist and said: "Doctor, I have a serious problem and desperately need your help! My baby is not even one year old and I'm pregnant again. I don't want kids so close together. So the doctor said: 'Ok and what do you want me to do? She said, 'I want you to end my pregnancy, and I 'm counting on your health with this'. The doctor thought for a little, and after some silence he said to the lady: 'I think I have a better solution for your problem. It's less dangerous for you too'. She smiled, thinking that the doctor was going to accept her request. Then he continued: 'You see, in order for you not to have to take care two babies at the same time, let's kill the one in your arms. This way, you could rest some before the other one is born. If we're going to kill one of them, it doesn't matter which one it is. There would be no risk for your body if you chose the one in your arms'.

The lady was horrified and said: 'No doctor! How terrible! It's a crime to kill a child! 'I agree', the doctor replied. 'But you seemed to be ok with it, so I thought maybe that was the best solution'. The doctor smiled, realizing that he had made his point. He convinced the mom that there is no difference in killing a child that's already been born and one that's still in the womb. The crime is the same!

"Love says I sacrifice myself for the good of the other person. Abortion says I sacrifice the other person for the good of myself…"

Chapter 83

Harmony (Black and White)

One of the most famous badges and coats of arms in the world is that of Achimota College in Ghana. It was designed and conceived by that great man, Aggrey.

Its pictures part of a key board of a piano with its black and white keys. And the symbolism is this: you can extract some kind of tune by playing only on the black keys, and you can do the same by using only the white keys. But to produce a real tune and real harmony, you must use both black and white notes to produce the best music and harmony.

Chapter 84

The Tired, the Contented, the Enthusiasts

Pierre Theilhard de Chardin once told the following story. A group of mountain climbers took off to scale the heights. After some hours of walking, about half way up and soon split up into three groups:

One group was sorry it had undertaken such a strenuous trip fraught with dangers and disproportionate to the expected enjoyment. So disheartened and tired, this group turned back.

The second group was happy to be here in the clear mountain air and with the sun tanning them. So they spread themselves out on the mountain grass and heartily ate the tasty sandwiches they had brought along. Some broke out into song and breathed in the freedom of the heights. They were content and happy right here. Why move on higher? So they stayed right there.

It was only the third group of real mountain climbers who took off for the summit, which they had kept before their eyes from the time they left the valley. That was their goal and they relished straining every muscle to attain it.

In life we climb our goal, at times we belong to one of these three groups.

Chapter 85

Providence of God

In the Northern part of Scotland is a very long railroad bridge passing over the firth of Jay. In the midst of a furious storm the speedy passenger train from Edinburgh passed onto the bridge in the middle of the night and completely disappeared. The accident was discovered only in the morning. No one ever knew exactly how many people lost their lives.

It so happened that just before the train went onto the bridge it made an unscheduled stop. One passenger went out onto the rear platform to get a few breaths of air. The stormy blast swept his hat off his head, and since the train was standing still, he jumped off and chased his rolling hat. Meanwhile, the train started up again and all he saw were two red lights disappeared into the storm.

There were no houses in the area so he had to find shelter as best he could near the road... complaining all night long over his bad luck. Then in the morning he found out that he was the only passenger on that train who had not lost his life. He stopped complaining and saw it as God's way.

Chapter 86

Handicaps

A doctor spoke to the young mother of a tiny baby: 'I am very sorry, Mrs. Keller, but you must be brave. Prepare yourself for a severe shock". With tears in her eyes and trembling lips the mother asked, "Then my baby is not going to get better? She is going to…."

She was so heartbroken that she could not finish. The doctor anticipated her question, 'No, she is not going to die, but she will be both blind and deaf". In anguish she exclaimed, "Blind and deaf, Oh, my poor Helen, what will become of you?" "What indeed", echoed the doctor who muttered to himself as he left the room. "It's a sad case; one of the worst I have ever attended and the baby might as well be dead".

The baby grew up to be known as Helen Keller, one of the most famous, useful and happy person. Depending upon the sense of touch and of smell, she learned laboriously to speak and then to write. Her story spread and she was invited to speak to groups throughout the world. She finished high school and college and has authored a number of inspiring books.

Chapter 87

Honesty

A young lad knocked on the door of a lady's house and asked if she would like to buy some of the berries he had just picked. 'Yes", she said, "and I'll take your pail in the kitchen and measure out two quarts".

The boy stood outside and played with the dog. 'Why don't you come in and see that I measure your berries right?' inquired the lady. 'How do you know that I won't cheat you?"

"I am not afraid", replied the lad, "for you would get the worst of it".

"What do you mean by that?" the lady asked.

"Why Ma'am," said the boy, "I would only lose the berries; but you would make yourself a thief.

Chapter 88

A Crippled Baby

After 20 years of childless marriage, the couple's joy knew no bounds when they learned that a baby was on the way. But on the day of the delivery the doctor's heart ached to see that the infant had only a tiny stump of a left arm. He steeled himself to tell the father and offered to break the news to the mother. "No", said the father sturdily, 'I want to tell her myself ".

Together they placed the swathed baby by the mother's side. She admired the soft skin, traced the hairline with her fingers and looked proudly at her husband, "She's perfect, isn't she?

Something in her husband's eyes warned her. Slowly she removed the blankets and saw the crippled arm. The room was very quiet. Then she turned again to her husband and said softly, "John, the Lord knew just where to send this baby, didn't he? He understood how much we needed her and how much she needs us".

Chapter 89

Fatherhood

A devoted father was ushered into the hospital room where his seven year old son was at death's door from an incurable disease. The lad seemed to sense that he would not get well.

He said, "Dad, am I going to die?"

"Why do you ask, son? Are you afraid to die?"

Looking up with trusting eyes, the boy replied; 'Not if God is like you, Daddy".

Chapter 90

Making Time for Prayer

As the pastor was taking up the census in his parish he asked of one family the routine question, "Do you have kind of family prayer at any time? " "Oh, Father", answered the head of the house, "We just don't have time for it"

The priest asked, "Suppose you knew that one of your children would take sick if you did not pray together. Would you have some kind of family prayer?" "Oh, I guess we would", answered the father of the family.

"Suppose you knew that on the day when you failed to have a family prayer, one of your children would be injured in an accident, would you pray together?" Again came the answer. "We certainly would".

"Suppose", went on the priest, "that every day you failed to say a prayer together, the law would fine you five dollars. Would you neglect to pray?" "I am sure we would pray, Father. But what's the idea of all these questions?"

"Just this", explained the priest, "Your problem is not time. You could find time. The problem is that you don't think family prayer is important, as important as paying a fine or keeping your children healthy. The blessing of God won through prayer is more important than anything else you can think of".

Chapter 91

Ready for Death

A steamer laden with passengers was making the round of South America and ran into a sand bar. The high waves beat against the crippled ship and it began to sink. A small schooner appeared in the distant horizon and its signals brought it to the rescue. But it was too small to hold all the passengers. So off went the women and children first. Lots were cast among the men for who must go and who must stay.

Among the men aboard were two relatives, a catholic Lawyer named Burdette and his irreligious son-in-law Burdette drew the lucky card, his son-in-law the unlucky one. Mr. Burdette turned to the young man and said, "Take this card and save your life. I am a catholic and went to confession and received communion just before starting out on this trip. I am prepared to die. As for you, I have my doubts. Take this card and save your life".

It would be interesting to know how the young man used his SECOND LIFE.

Chapter 92

Complaining to God

History tells us of one of the Caesars who prepared a great feast to which many were invited. At the appointed time, a great storm threatened and no one arrived. In anger with the "storm God", Caesar had his soldiers shoot arrows into the sky as revenge.

The shower of arrows fell back to earth to inflict injuries on many of the soldiers while Jupiter, the fictitious God, was unharmed. Our murmurings are like so many arrows shot towards God. They will only return to bring us harm.

Chapter 93

Values in and Near You

A South African farmer, who had been trying for years to eke out a living from the dry rock soil of his farm, finally gave up. He'd heard that people were finding diamonds all over the country, so he sold his farm and set out to look for diamonds.

After a year of fruitless searching, he died penniless and in despair. One day, the man to whom he had sold the farm noticed some unusual rocks in a corner of a field. Curious, he took them into his kitchen and washed them off, then polished them.

That farm turned out to be the first Kimberly diamond mine.

Chapter 94

Selfless Love

My wife called, "How long will you be with that newspaper? Will you come here and make your darling daughter eat her food?" I tossed the paper away and rushed to the scene. My only daughter, Sindu, looked frightened; tears were welling up in her eyes. In front of her was a bowl filled to its brim with curd rice. Sindu is a nice girl, quite intelligent for her age. I cleared my throat and picked up the bowl. "Sindu, darling, why don't you take a few mouthful of this curd rice? Just for dad's sake, dear." Sindu softened a bit and wiped her tears with the back of her hands. "Ok, Dad. I will eat – not just a few mouthfuls, but the whole lot of this. But you should…." Sindu hesitated. "Dad, if I eat this entire curd rice, will you give me whatever I ask for? "Promise." I covered the pink softened hand extended by my daughter with mine and clinched the deal. Now I became a bit anxious. "Sindu, dear, you shouldn't insist on getting a computer or any such expensive items. Dad does not have that kind of money right now. Ok?" "No. dad I do not want anything expensive." Slowly and painfully she finished eating the whole quantity. I was silently angry with my wife and my mother for forcing my child to eat something that she detested.

After the ordeal was through, Sindu came to me with her eyes wise with expectation. All our attention was on her. "Dad, I want to have my head shaved off, this Sunday!" was her demand. "Atrocious!" shouted my wife, "A girl child having her head shaved off." Impossible!

"Never in our family!" my mother rasped. "She has been watching too much of television. Our culture is getting totally spoiled with these TV programs! "Sindu, darling why don't you ask for something else? We will be sad seeing you with a clean-shaven head." "Please, Sindu, why don't you try to understand our feelings?" I tried to plead with her. 'Dad, you saw how difficult it was for me to eat that curd rice.' Sindu was in tears. 'And you promised to grant me whatever I ask for. Now, you are going back on your words. Was it not you who told me the story of King Harish

Chandra and its moral that we should honor our promises no matter what?

It was time for me to call the shots. 'Our promise must be kept.' Are you out of your mind chorused my mother and wife. 'No, if we go back on our promises, she will never learn to honor her own. Sindu, your wish will be fulfilled. With her head clean shaven, Sindu had a round face, and her eyes looked big and beautiful.

On Monday morning, I dropped her at her school. It was a sight to watch my hairless Sindu walking towards her classroom. She turned around and waved. I waved back with a smile. Just then, a boy alighted from a car, and shouted, 'Sinduja, please wait for me!' what struck me was the hairless head of that boy. 'May be that is the in-stuff', I thought. 'Sir, your daughter Sinduja is great indeed!' without introducing herself, a lady got out of her car and continued, 'that boy who is walking along with your daughter is my son Harish. He is suffering from Leukemia." She paused to muffle her sobs. 'Harish could not attend the school for the whole of the last month. He lost all his hair due to the side effect of the Chemotherapy. He refused to come back to school fearing the unintentional but cruel teasing of the school mates. Sinduja visited him last week, and promised him that she will take care of the teasing issue. But, I never imagined she would sacrifice her lovely hair for the sake of my son.' Sir you and your wife are blessed to have such a noble soul as your daughter. 'I stood transfixed and then, I wept. My little angel, you are teaching me how selfless real love is!'

Chapter 95

Small Beginnings

A Kansas farmer returned from his field one day and found a very small potato in his pocket. Jokingly, he handed it to his twelve-year-old nephew who was visiting them. "Here", he said, "Plant that here on my farm and you can have all the potatoes you raise from it until you are 21 years old".

The boy was bright. He cut the potato into as many pieces as it had "eyes" and planted the pieces behind the barn. That autumn he dug up his potatoes, put them aside, and next spring cut his potatoes, and made another planting. His crop did very well from year to year, and his fourth year's harvest was over one hundred bushels. The farmers saw that the boy's planting would soon cover all his land. So he begged to be freed from his hasty offer.

Of course, he was willing, since he had made quite a profit from that one small potato already.

Big things grow from small beginnings.

Chapter 96

Motive-Conviction

A general decided to attack even though he was outnumbered ten to one. He was sure he would win, but his soldiers were full of doubts.

So on the way to battle, he stopped at a shrine and went in and said some prayers. When he came back outside, he told the soldiers, "I am going to toss a coin. If it is heads we shall win." "If it is tails, we shall lose. Destiny will now reveal her hand".

He tossed the coin. It was heads. The soldiers were so eager to fight that they won the battle easily.

The next day, one of the lesser officers with great conviction told the general, "That just goes to show that no one can change the hand of destiny".

"Quite right", said the general, showing him that the coin had heads on both sides.

Chapter 97

That's Life

A poor boy was in love with a rich man's daughter. One day the boy proposed to her and the girl said, "Hey! Listen, your monthly salary is my daily expense. How can I be involved with you….? How could you have thought of that? I can never love you, so forget about me and get engaged to someone else of your level." But somehow the boy could not forget her so easily.

Sometime 10 years later they stumbled into each other in a shopping mall. The lady again said "Hey….! You! How are you? Now I'm married and do you know how much my husband's salary is ….? $15700 per month! Can you beat that? And he is also very smart." The guy's eyes got wet with tears on hearing those words from the same lady…

A few seconds later, her husband came around but before the lady could say a word her husband seeing the guy said…. "Sir you're here and you've met my wife…" then he said to his wife, "this is my boss. I'm also one of those working on his $100 million project! And do you know a fact, my dear?"

My boss loved a lady but he couldn't win her heart…that's why he has remained unmarried since. How lucky would that lady have been, if she had married my boss now? These days, who would love someone that much?" He said all this to his wife.

The lady stood in total shock but couldn't utter a word.

Chapter 98

A Box of Food Gifts A Wedding Ring

There was a poor boy named Roy Freetz in a 30 student classroom who was really hungry and had nothing to eat. He felt jealous about all of his classmates, for they were eating and enjoying their food.

He was standing in one of the corners of the room. There was a girl, who came to him and gave all the food that was in her box.

The boy was surprised and tried to refuse it but the girl had already left the place. She left not only the class room but also stopped studying and went to another town.

Many years had passed; the girl was working as a meat vendor in the town. There was a time when she was going to the market, when she was hit by a car and was seriously injured, and had to be hospitalized.

The doctor did everything to save her. After sleeping for five days, she woke up and felt miserable for her family for they had no money to pay the hospital bill.

The nurse came and gave the hospital bill. It was stated: "Everything is paid by one box of food for the past many years." Signed by Roy Freetz.

The girl cried and thanked everyone in the room and when she looked at the back of the paper there it was written in bold, "WILL YOU MARRY ME?"

The doctor came and gave the ring. The girl accepted the proposal joyfully.

Chapter 99

Is there Love after Death?

Richard was 19 almost. He was intelligent and smart too. Everyone loved him. Not only because he was loveable but also because he suffered from cancer. Cancer, an undesirable and evil disease that can't be treated. Richard was just a guest for few months. No one knew what might happen in any time.

His mother took care of him a lot. Anyway she was a mother. Every mother loves her child. Richard never used to go out from home; he always used to be with his mother. He used to pass time watching, television, playing video games, and so on. He always admired to go out of home and wanted to see the world. He used to wonder how's the life outside home? How the environment is outside home? How are the people? And so on. One day he asked permission to go out of home and his mother gave.

He was walking through the pavement wondering about the city. He passed through many shops. Suddenly, his glance went on a girl sitting in a reception in a big audio parlor. He saw her and began looking at her as she did to. They were looking at each other. It seemed as if they knew each other since ages. He went to the shop and approached the girl. "May I help you? Asked the girl he was nervous. "Oh yes I need a CD," said Richard. She smiled with gentle charm on her face and said "Which one? Ammm!! I mean whose record?" Hmm!! Lobo. "Which Album?"she asked. "Any" he replied. She picked a record of Lobo and went back door and came out with a CD packed. He began to like that girl and started to go there every day. He bought a CD every day. But didn't even the pack. Every day the girl picked the CD she liked and went backdoor and came out with CD packed. One day, when the girl went backdoor, he left a piece of paper below the money where he wrote his phone number and his name and came back home taking the CD.

Ring!! Ring!! Telephone buzzed. "Hello," said mother. "May I talk to

Richard please?" Then his mother started crying. She wept till her eyes were dry and said, "He passed away yesterday." And kept the receiver.

The next day as Richards's remembrance bothered her a lot; she went to his room and started watching his clothes, shoes etc. as she opened the cupboard she found packs of CD's along with many pills and medicines. She opened one by one. As she opened the first, there was a piece of paper. It said, "You are cute. Do you wanna friendship with me?" the other pieces of paper said "Hey! You are really cute. You know, you really impressed me." The other said, "Why aren't you replying me? You know I am gonna crazy 'about you. And I think I am gonna love you."

And all the rest said

"I love you"

Chapter 100

True Love

This is what True Love is all about: it was a busy morning, approximately 8.30 a.m. when an elderly gentleman in his 80's arrived to have stitches removed from his thumb. He stated that he was in a hurry as he had an appointment at 9.00 a.m. I took his vital signs and had him take a seat, knowing it would be over an hour before someone would be able to see him. I saw him look at his watch and decided, since I was not busy with another patient, I would evaluate his wound. On examining it, I found it well healed. So I talked to one of the doctors, got the needed supplies to remove his stitches and redressed his wound. While taking care of his wound, we began to engage in conversation. I asked him if he had another doctor's appointment this morning, as he was in such a hurry. The gentleman told me no, and that he needed to go to the nursing home to eat breakfast with his wife. I, then, inquired as to her health. He told me that she had been there for a while and that she was a victim of Alzheimer's disease. As we talked I asked if she would be upset if he was a bit late. He replied that she no longer knew who he was, that she had not recognized him in five years now. I was surprised, and asked him, "And you still go every morning, even though she doesn't know who you are?" He smiled as he patted my hand and said, "She doesn't know me, but I still know who she is". I had to hold back tears as he left, I had goose bumps on my arm, and thought, "That is the kind of love I want in my life".

www.ingramcontent.com/pod-product-compliance
Lightning Source LLC
LaVergne TN
LVHW041110150826
845673LV00007B/1990

* 9 7 9 8 8 9 6 7 3 8 9 2 3 *